The Tenth Chester Book of Motets

The Italian and Spanish Schools for 5 voices

Edited by Anthony G. Petti

LIST OF MOTETS

CHESTER MUSIC

Cover:
Virgin and Child in a landscape. Netherlandish School.
Presented by Queen Victoria to the National Gallery
at the Prince Consort's wish in 1863
Reproduced by courtesy of the Trustees,
The National Gallery, London.

DOMINATOR COELORUM

Ruler of the heavens and creator of the earth, who has destroyed war from the beginning, raise your arm over the peoples who intend evil against your servants, and let your justice be glorified in us. (Cf. *Judith* ix, 10-11).
Alto cantus firmus: Give peace in our days, O Lord, for there is no one else but you, Our God, who may fight for us.

Costanzo Festa (c.1480-1545)

ADORAMUS TE CHRISTE

We adore you, Christ, and we bless you, because by your holy cross you have redeemed the world.

Giovanni Maria Nanino (c. 1543-1607)

9

O BEATA TRINITAS

O holy and blessed Trinity, the Father, Son and Holy Spirit, alleluia.
O holy and glorious unity, the Father, Son and Holy Spirit, alleluia.

G. P. da Palestrina (1525-94)

16

VOCE MEA

I have called to the Lord with my voice: I have pleaded with the Lord with my voice. I pour out my supplication.
in his presence; I speak of my misery before him. Hear, O Lord, the voice of my petition when I pray to you
(Ps. 142, i-ii).

Costanzo Porta (1529-1601)

18

MIRABILE MYSTERIUM

A wonderful mystery is made known today: nature is renewed; God has become man; that which was remains, and that which did not exist has been taken on; He has undergone neither a mixing nor a division.

Pietro Vinci (c.1530-84)

* Tenor and Quintus have been interchanged for bars 1-10 and 38, iii to the end.

REPLETI SUNT OMNES

They were all filled with the Holy Spirit and began to speak, alleluia (*Acts,* ii, 4).

Juan Esquivel (late 16th-early 17th cent.)

26

*Alto and Tenor can be interchanged from here to 25, i.

MANUS TUAE DOMINE

Your hands have made me and have shaped me completely: will you suddenly destroy me? Remember that you have made me out of clay and will return me to dust. Did you not pour me out like milk and curdle me like cheese? You clothed me in skin and flesh: you did knit me together with bones and sinews. You granted me life and your mercy, and your care has preserved my spirit (*Job,* x, 8-12).

Cristobal Morales (c. 1500-53)

30

GLORIA LAUS

Glory, praise and honour to you, Christ, Redeemer King, to whom the children sang their glad hosannas. You are the King of Israel, of David's royal lineage: a blessed King, you come in the name of the Lord.

Juan Ginés Perez (1548-1612)

36

GAUDE VIRGO MARIA

Rejoice, Virgin Mary: you alone have destroyed all heresies in the whole world, alleluia.

Tomás Luis de Victoria(c.1548-1611)

The aim of this present series is to make available a comprehensive body of Latin motets from the Renaissance and Early Baroque periods, combining old favourites with lesser known or hitherto unpublished works. Generally speaking, all the pieces are within the scope of the reasonably able choir. They also encompass a fair selection from the liturgical year as a guide for use both in church and in the concert hall when performing choirs wish to present their programme according to theme or a particular season.

The editor has endeavoured to preserve a balance between a critical and performing edition. The motets are, where necessary, transposed into the most practical performing keys, are barred, fully underlayed, and provided with breathing marks. They also have a reduction either as a rehearsal aid or as a form of accompaniment, since at least some of the works of the later period were clearly intended to be reinforced by a continuo. Generally speaking, note values are halved in duple time, and quartered in triple time. Editorial tempi and dynamics are supplied only in the reduction, leaving choirmasters free to supply their own in the light of their interpretation of a given piece, vocal resources and the acoustics. The vocal range is given at the beginning of each motet. Also provided is a translation of every text and a table of use.

As an aid to musicologists, the motets are transcribed, wherever possible, from the most authoritative sources, and the original clefs, signatures and note values are given at the beginning and wherever they change during the course of a piece. Ligatures are indicated by slurs, editorial accidentals are placed above the stave, and the underlay is shown in italics when it expands a ditto sign, or in square brackets if editorial. When the original contains a basso continuo, it is included as the bass line of the reduction. Figurings are not included, however, because they are extremely sparse, and do not normally indicate any more than the harmony already provided by the vocal parts. Finally, each volume includes a brief introduction concerning the scope of the edition, with notes on the composers, the motets, and the sources, together with a list of editorial emendations and alterations, if any.

This volume contains nine motets from the 16th and early 17th centuries, five of them by Italian composers and the remaining four by Spanish. As with all of the volumes from nine to twelve in this series, the fifth voice is for soprano (occasionally mezzo soprano), because this combination is probably the easiest for the average choir to accommodate.

Five-part motets are not especially numerous in the first part of the 16th century, but are prevalent towards the end, possibly as part of the trend towards the polychoral writings so much in vogue in the Early Baroque period. The fifth voice (often called Quintus or Quinta Vox) is generally drawn from the lower parts. However, as if in imitation of madrigal style, the habit of using as the fifth voice a second cantus equal with cantus one and often in canon with it gradually comes into fashion by the end of the 16th century.

The first and earliest composer in this volume, Costanzo Festa (c.1480-1545), was one of the few Italians to make headway in his own country at a time when Flemish composers held a virtual monopoly. He was born in Piedmont, but travelled south to Rome, where in 1517 he became a member of the Papal choir at one of the most glorious eras in its history, and became chapel master there until his death. Festa's compositions are copious both in secular music (he was supreme in the three-part madrigal) and in sacred music, his works including four masses, forty motets, and thirty Vesper hymns. Some of his music survives in the Biblioteca Vallicelliana, Rome, as does the present example, *Dominator caelorum* (Cod. Borromini, E. II, 55-60, N. 16; another copy of which survives in the Cathedral Library, Padua Co.d. D, 27, ff.78-80).

That a motet to be sung in time of war has been selected for this volume does not reflect editorial pessimism, but a limitation of choice for Festa in this particular five-part combination, and the will to include a relatively uncommon text. Most importantly, this is a fine work, emotionally controlled, clean cut, simply conceived, and with a pleasing sense of direction. One of its notable features is the use, in late 15th century Flemish style, of a delayed *cantus firmus* with a totally different text and melody from the other parts, which also develops from a simple plainsong line in augmentation to a swiftly moving and ornamented melody (e.g., bars 46-52). The mode is appropriate and secure, being Hypodorian with inevitable modulation into the Hypoaeolian because of the frequent flattened G's (as transposed). Festa nicely combines homophony for the opening invocation with compact and almost monosyllabic fugues of supplication, in which, in rhetorical repetition, much the same subject is used for every point. The motet also contains some of Festa's characteristic features: the two-note turn (e.g. S I, bars 4, 11, 14, 42, 50) and liberal parallel thirds, sixths and tenths (e.g., bars 4, 9, 15, 19, etc.). Also to be noted is the restrained but effective word-painting, where, for "eleva brachium" there is a clarion rise up the triad to the top of the register in all parts that have the text.

Giovanni Maria Nanino (or Nanini), not to be confused with his younger brother, Giovanni Bernardino, was a disciple of Palestrina. Like Festa, he sang as well as composed. After his early days as a choirboy in Vallerano, he went to Rome and became a singer at Santa Maria Maggiore, succeeding Palestrina there as maestro di cappella in 1571. He then held a similar post at San Luigi de' Francesi (1575-7), and in 1604 became director of music at the Sistine Chapel. He also founded a music school with the aid of his brother and Palestrina.

Like most composers of the period, even those in holy orders, Nanino wrote madrigals and canzonets as well as a fairly large body of sacred music, which comprises mainly motets and psalms. Somewhat of a traditionalist, he is preoccupied in his sacred music with the different ways of employing a cantus firmus, and even wrote 157 settings of a cantus firmus by Festa,– whose style he markedly imitates, as can be seen by comparing their two works in this volume. One of Nanino's favourite ways of employing the cantus firmus is by different forms of canon, at which he is a master. However, he does not use this style in one of his most famous motets, *Diffusa est gratia,* or in the present example, *Adoramus te Christe* (Vatican Library, Cappella Sistina, ms., cod. 484-8).

There is no cantus firmus in this work, and canons appear only sporadically (e.g., S II and tenor, bars 2-10), though fugal imitation is fairly extended. Most settings of this highly popular text are either predominantly homophonic (e.g., Rosselli's, formerly ascribed to Palestriana, and Ruffo's), or save the fugue until "quia per sanctam crucem" (e.g., Lassus's setting in volume 7 of this series). By contrast, Nanino begins with a well-aired fugue and becomes noticeably chordal only by the second "et benedicimus" (bar 15), with the usual ornaments and melisma for "tibi". The modulations are skilful, and mode and key combine well (as the opening bars amply illustrate). As might be expected, a series of major chords are introduced for "redemisti" (cf. the Lassus setting) and for the conclusion. Vocal combinations are skilfully varied, providing not only a range of tonal colour, but also a sense of antiphony and gradual climax, as in "quia per sanctam crucem" (bars 24-34), which moves from the three lowest voices to an answer in the four top voices, and then to a tutti for "redemisti", a technique repeated in the final section (bars 39ff.).

The life of the greatest 16th century Italian composer, Giovanni Pierluigi da Palestrina (c.1525-94) is fortunately very well documented: it is also one of the few lives of musicians thought appropriate for an opera, since it is rich and varied, contains many setbacks, and includes two marriages, for one of which he renounced his priestly vows. Palestrina spent most of his musical life in Rome, and held several important positions: as chapel master of the Julian choir, then of St. John Lateran and St. Maria Maggiore, though a plan to make him chapel master of the Pontifical Choir under Sixtus V proved abortive. His range of publications is formidable, including ninety four masses, about four hundred motets, twelve lamentations and no fewer than thirty settings of the magnificat. Even more amazing is the uniformly high standard that runs throughout his works, though he nods occasionally, as in some of his masses. Five-part motets are especially popular with Palestrina, since he provided at least one hundred and seventy four.

The *O beata,* part one of a double motet (part two is *O vera summa*), was first published in *Liber primus mottettorum quae partim quinis, partim senis, partim septenis vocibus concinantur,* Rome, 1569 (complete set in the Staatsbibliothek, Berlin, Bundesrepublik). It is a work of great brilliance, but also has a warmth, tenderness and delicacy which are almost more apt for a motet to the Virgin than to the Trinity. Most of the vibrancy comes from the two equally matched soprano parts, which are constantly capping one another, and dictate the mood and the pace almost from the very opening of the apostrophe of wonderment, to the passages of devout meditation and the lively dances of praise in the alleluia sections. The alto, too, has a prominent part and leads the opening fugue of invocation, but the tenor has mainly a supporting role, and the bass is used very sparingly, with entries mainly at climaxes. Palestrina's fairly strict adherence to the Lydian mode, with the E♭ rarely in evidence, contributes considerably to the work's remarkable etherial quality. This is surely one of the loveliest yet most exciting motets that the Renaissance ever produced.

The next composer, Costanzo Porta (1529-1601), unlike the preceding three, is not a member of the Roman School, but studied with Adrian Willaert at St. Mark's, Venice. A Franciscan monk, Porta quickly became celebrated as a choirmaster, holding that position first at Osimo, neat Ancona, and then at the great Franciscan church of St. Antony of Padua (the Cappella Antoniana). He was also intermittently maestro di cappella at the cathedral in Ravenna and at the Santa Casa di Loreto. His sacred music is very copious, and includes masses, motets, psalms, hymns and introits. As might be expected of a talented pupil of Willaert, Porta's work combines Flemish skill in counterpoint with Venetian sonority.

This is true to some extent of his *Voce mea* (manuscript copy in the Conservatorio di Musica G. B. Martini, Bologna, Cod. Q. 28) which also has some of the angularity that is to be found in penitential motets of Lassus (e.g., the *Improperium,* volume five of this series). Especially effective yet remarkably simple is the use of a semitone fall at the end of many of the phrases as a touch of wistfulness and yearning (e.g., Soprano I, bars 4-5, 9-10, 25, 32-3, 42-3). Most of the melodic phrases have a haunting and chantlike quality, especially in the Soprano I, making all the more effective the use of repetition as an intensification of the pleading (S I, bars 3-8, 32-47). The whole fabric of the motet is remarkably subtle, and the technique of free imitation is neither facile nor easy to predict, yet always seems remarkably fitting. As might be expected, the mode is Aeolian, with frequent incursions into A minor, but the customary note of optimism is heard in the final A major chord.

Pietro Vinci is comparatively neglected, yet his music is extremely expressive and eloquent. He was born in Nicosia, Sicily c.1530. What little is known of his life indicates that he was a well-respected maestro di cappella, holding this position in the church of Santa Maria Maggiore at Bergamo during the 1570s and, in 1581, a similar position in the city of his birth. He died in or around 1584. His compositions include madrigals, masses and motets. His *Mirabile mysterium (Il secondo libro de motetti a cinque voci,* 1572, Conservatorio, Bologna) seems in many ways traditional, especially in its use of imitation and harmony, certainly by contrast with Jacob Handl's setting. Yet it is an individual work, and makes its impact by the smoothness, sonority and economic force of its phrases. These qualities are apparent from the very beginning, which is comparable in effect to the opening of Victoria's *O magnum mysterium* (volume 3 in this series). The general mood of the piece is one of sustained awe, carried through to the final Phrygian cadence in a predominantly Aeolian mode.

Juan Esquivel, the first of the Spanish composers represented here, flourished at the beginning of the 17th century. He was a pupil of Juan Navarro, and succeeded him as chapel master at Ciudad Rodrigo. He was patronised by the bishop of that diocese, Pedro Ponce de Leon, who subsidised his publications, which included a volume of masses (1608), motets for four, five, six and eight voices (1608), a lost volume of psalms, hymns, antiphons and masses (1613). Works also survive in manuscript.

Esquivel's *Repleti sunt omnes* was first published in *Motecta festorum et dominicarum,* 1608 (copy in the Library of the Hispanic Society of America). Though it is not an especially remarkable motet, it is workmanlike, compact and effective. The opening fugue is forceful and orderly, moving down the voices, as each in turn responds to the Holy Spirit. There follows a short attractive and very brief fugue for "et coeperunt loqui", but most attention is paid to the final alleluia, which is half the length of the whole piece and contains a sequential set of mainly rising, lively and melodious figures, as if the main point of receiving the gift of speech is to sound the praises of God.

The "most excellent" Cristobal Morales (c.1500-53) is only now being given the attention befitting his deserts. Among his early appointments were the posts of chapel master at Ávila and then Plasencia. In the early 1530s he left for

Rome, becoming a singer in the Papal chapel. He was back in Spain by 1545, when he obtained the coveted post of chapel master at Toledo Cathedral, though he stayed only a short time. He then went to Marchena in Andalusia, where he was patronised by the Duke of Arcos (1548-51), and his final post was at Málaga. Morales concentrated almost entirely on sacred music, his compositions including twenty one masses, a set of Lamentations, the Office of the Dead, and motets, many of which remained unpublished.

The *Manus tuae Domine* was not published in Morales's lifetime, surviving in manuscript in the monastery of the Escorial (book 5, ff. 72v. -4). It is a powerful motet with an almost profound sense of suffering. The polyphony is masterly. The cantus parts sing in exact canon throughout, and the piece begins with every part in a soulful canon in the unusual Phrygian mode (the alto entering at the fifth), though this is an implied dominant to the Aeolian mode or A minor. The phrases are beautifully balanced and match the force of utterance and accentuation of the words without any use of wordpainting. However, dissonances are abundant, some of them unprepared and thickly clustered.

Jaun Ginéz Perez was born in Orihuela, Murcia, in 1548, and died there in 1612. He was a royal chaplain, and for a time maestro di cappella at Valencia. His music is wide-ranging and often includes such Early Baroque features as the use of a continuo, and the alternation of solo voice with polyphony. The *Gloria laus* (which, like many other motets by Perez, survives in a manuscript collection in Valencia Cathedral), is not, however, Early Baroque in any way, but neither is it especially traditional. For example, the plainsong melody of this famous hymn does not feature as a cantus firmus (cf. Tye's setting in volume two of this series), though clearly it provides some of the thematic material, notably at "Rex Christe" and, more obviously and extensively, at "Israel es tu Rex". The work has a very rich texture and is crowded with movement in every part. Barely any prolonged rest is given to any part except at the beginning of the second strophe: clearly the hymn of praise has to be as full-throated as possible for the triumphal Palm Sunday procession.

The last composer in this volume, Tomás Luis de Victoria (c.1548-1611), is the greatest Spanish composer of the 16th century, even though his output is comparatively small, and is exclusively sacred music. He was born at Ávila and entered the cathedral there as a choirboy around 1558. He also probably attended the Jesuit boys' school of St. Giles, which was patronised by St. Teresa of Ávila. In 1565 he went to Rome, and by 1573 was music instructor at the German College and maestro di cappella at the Seminario Romano, as well as music director at Santa Maria di Monserrato. Victoria returned to Spain by about 1587, becoming chaplain to the Dowager Empress at the Royal Convent in Madrid until her death in 1603, and choirmaster to the choir of priests and boys attached to the convent. Victoria's compositions include masses, motets, psalms, magnificats, the Office of the Dead, and the Office of Holy Week. The relative modesty of output is amply compensated for by remarkable range and profundity.

Victoria wrote hardly any five-part motets suitable for SSATB, and what there is certainly makes one wish he had written many more. *Gaude Virgo Maria* was first published as no. 23 of *Motecta*, Venice, 1572, a popular collection reprinted five times (present transcription from 1585 edition, copy in Christ Church College, Oxford). It is a gentle and joyous work of great delicacy. The two soprano parts sing a shapely and ornamented cantus firmus in canon, while the other parts weave their mellifluous patterns in free imitation. The final alleluia, with the undulating four-quaver figure repeated in each part, has a grace and beauty which readily demonstrate why Victoria is one of the masters of Renaissance polyphony.

Editorial emendations and alterations.

O beata, A, 54, D altered from F.
Mirabile mysterium, Tenor and Quintus switched from 1-10 and 38, iii to the end.

Table of use according to the Tridentine Rite

Motet	Liturgical source	Seasonal or festal use
Dominator coelorum	partly antiphon for peace (Da pacem)	time of war, general
Adoramus te Christe	antiphon, Good Friday service	Good Friday, Lent, general
O beata Trinitas	Office of Trinity	Trinity Sunday, general
Voce mea	psalm, Friday Vespers; Holy Saturday Vespers; All Souls, Compline	Lent, general
Mirabile mysterium		Christmas, Corpus Christi, Communion
Repleti sunt omnes	3rd antiphon, 2nd Vespers, Pentecost	Pentecost, Holy Spirit
Manus tuae Dominae	3rd lesson, Office of the Dead	Funerals, Lent
Gloria laus	hymn, procession of palms, Palm Sunday	Palm Sunday, Christ the King
Gaude Virgo Maria		Blessed Virgin

I wish to acknowledge the assistance of my wife and Marian Žekulin in checking the proofs of this volume.